This Romans study workbook is intended [to help you] deep dive into Scripture on your own without devotional leading questions. Instead, there are blank dot grid pages for writing questions and observations. Following each chapter are special sections to record your answers to the following study questions:

Who? *Who is speaking? Who is being addressed? Who is present? Who is active in the passage? Who is being spoken about or acted towards?*

What? *What is being said, or what action is taking place?*

Where? *What is the location of the action or dialogue? Zoom in and out here. Whose house? What city? What nation?*

When? *When is this dialogue or action taking place? Time of day? Time of week? Time of year? What happened just prior?*

Why? *What is the purpose of the dialogue or action? What is it in response to?*

Wherefore? *Why is this included in the Bible? What are we meant to learn or understand?*

These initial questions will encourage you to think deeply about all of the provided details in a given passage.

Dallas Theological Seminary *offers a free online course on How to Read the Bible Like a Seminary Professor that is really helpful for further explaining how to correctly interpret scripture using these criteria. I highly recommend you check it out! This workbook is not endorsed by DTS.*

The next section is meant to help you begin to interpret the passage correctly:

Content: *Make note of things like instructions given, special or curious details provided, comparisons made, lists, questions and answers, figures of speech, etc. You may choose to circle or underline them in the text before listing them here.*

Context: *What is the context within the scripture? Read what happens in the passages before and after the one you're studying in order to correctly ascertain the meaning.*

Comparison: *A concordance is helpful here! Compare it to similar passages of scripture, to events or conversations that happen in a similar time or place, or to passages in other parts of the bible, both New and Old Testament. Does this scripture passage ring a bell or make you think of something else? Use scripture to interpret scripture.*

Culture: *Time to do some homework. Using references like a bible atlas, discover everything you can about what cultural influences may be present in the passage including the original language, references to historical figures, references to cultural practices or customs, etc.*

Consultation: *Look up multiple commentaries on the passage you're studying to discover what you may have missed, help to illuminate difficult passages, and determine whether your own interpretation is on the right path.*

The version of Romans printed in this workbook is the WEB (World English Bible), a public domain translation.

1 Paul, a servant of Jesus Christ, called to be an apostle, set apart for the Good News of God, ² which he promised before through his prophets in the holy Scriptures, ³ concerning his Son, who was born of the offspring of David according to the flesh, ⁴ who was declared to be the Son of God with power, according to the Spirit of holiness, by the resurrection from the dead, Jesus Christ our Lord, ⁵ through whom we received grace and apostleship for obedience of faith among all the nations for his name's sake; ⁶ among whom you are also called to belong to Jesus Christ; ⁷ to all who are in Rome, beloved of God, called to be saints: Grace to you and peace from God our Father and the Lord Jesus Christ.

⁸ First, I thank my God through Jesus Christ for all of you, that your faith is proclaimed throughout the whole world. ⁹ For God is my witness, whom I serve in my spirit in the Good News of his Son, how unceasingly I make mention of you always in my prayers, ¹⁰ requesting, if by any means now at last I may be prospered by the will of God to come to you. ¹¹ For I long to see you, that I may impart to you some spiritual gift, to the end that you may be established; ¹² that is, that I with you may be encouraged in you, each of us by the other's faith, both yours and mine.

13 Now I don't desire to have you unaware, brothers, that I often planned to come to you, and was hindered so far, that I might have some fruit among you also, even as among the rest of the Gentiles. 14 I am debtor both to Greeks and to foreigners, both to the wise and to the foolish. 15 So as much as is in me, I am eager to preach the Good News to you also who are in Rome. 16 For I am not ashamed of the Good News of Christ, because it is the power of God for salvation for everyone who believes, for the Jew first, and also for the Greek. 17 For in it is revealed God's righteousness from faith to faith. As it is written, "But the righteous shall live by faith."

18 For the wrath of God is revealed from heaven against all ungodliness and unrighteousness of men who suppress the truth in unrighteousness, 19 because that which is known of God is revealed in them, for God revealed it to them. 20 For the invisible things of him since the creation of the world are clearly seen, being perceived through the things that are made, even his everlasting power and divinity, that they may be without excuse. 21 Because knowing God, they didn't glorify him as God, and didn't give thanks, but became vain in their reasoning, and their senseless heart was darkened.

For I am not ashamed of the Good News of Christ

²² Professing themselves to be wise, they became fools, ²³ and traded the glory of the incorruptible God for the likeness of an image of corruptible man, and of birds, four-footed animals, and creeping things. ²⁴ Therefore God also gave them up in the lusts of their hearts to uncleanness, that their bodies should be dishonored among themselves; ²⁵ who exchanged the truth of God for a lie, and worshiped and served the creature rather than the Creator, who is blessed forever. Amen.

²⁶ For this reason, God gave them up to vile passions. For their women changed the natural function into that which is against nature. ²⁷ Likewise also the men, leaving the natural function of the woman, burned in their lust toward one another, men doing what is inappropriate with men, and receiving in themselves the due penalty of their error. ²⁸ Even as they refused to have God in their knowledge, God gave them up to a reprobate mind, to do those things which are not fitting; ²⁹ being filled with all unrighteousness, sexual immorality, wickedness, covetousness, malice; full of envy, murder, strife, deceit, evil habits, secret slanderers, ³⁰ backbiters, hateful to God, insolent, arrogant, boastful, inventors of evil things, disobedient to parents, ³¹ without understanding, covenant breakers, without natural affection, unforgiving, unmerciful; ³² who, knowing the ordinance of God, that those who practice such things are worthy of death, not only do the same, but also approve of those who practice them.

WHY?
What led to the action or dialogue that took place in this passage? Record every question you have about the purpose for what is said or done.

OTHER QUESTIONS & OBSERVATIONS

CONTENT
Record figures of speech, questions and answers, lists, comparisons, etc. What questions do these bring up?

_____
_____
_____
_____
_____
_____
_____
_____
_____

CONTEXT
What is the immediate context and the broader context? What happens right before and after this passage?

_____
_____
_____
_____
_____
_____

COMPARISON
Track down scripture quotations, compare similar passages, notice other uses in scripture of special terms, names, or ideas.

_____
_____
_____
_____
_____
_____
_____

CULTURE
How does the cultural context influence this passage? What questions do you need answered about the culture to understand it better?

_____
_____
_____
_____
_____
_____
_____
_____
_____
_____

CONSULTATION
Explore commentaries and sermons on this passage and record helpful thoughts.

_____
_____
_____
_____
_____
_____
_____
_____
_____
_____
_____
_____
_____
_____

APPLICATION
Keeping in mind the meaning of this passage in its original context, how can you apply this passage to your life?

2 Therefore you are without excuse, O man, whoever you are who judge. For in that which you judge another, you condemn yourself. For you who judge practice the same things. ² We know that the judgment of God is according to truth against those who practice such things. ³ Do you think this, O man who judges those who practice such things, and do the same, that you will escape the judgment of God? ⁴ Or do you despise the riches of his goodness, forbearance, and patience, not knowing that the goodness of God leads you to repentance? ⁵ But according to your hardness and unrepentant heart you are treasuring up for yourself wrath in the day of wrath, revelation, and of the righteous judgment of God; ⁶ who "will pay back to everyone according to their works:" ⁷ to those who by perseverance in well-doing seek for glory, honor, and incorruptibility, eternal life; ⁸ but to those who are self-seeking, and don't obey the truth, but obey unrighteousness, will be wrath, indignation, ⁹ oppression, and anguish on every soul of man who does evil, to the Jew first, and also to the Greek.

¹⁰ But glory, honor, and peace go to every man who does good, to the Jew first, and also to the Greek. ¹¹ For there is no partiality with God.

¹² For as many as have sinned without the law will also perish without the law. As many as have sinned under the law will be judged by the law. ¹³ For it isn't the hearers of the law who are righteous before God, but the doers of the law will be justified ¹⁴ (for when Gentiles who don't have the law do by nature the things of the law, these, not having the law, are a law to themselves, ¹⁵ in that they show the work of the law written in their hearts, their conscience testifying with them, and their thoughts among themselves accusing or else excusing them) ¹⁶ in the day when God will judge the secrets of men, according to my Good News, by Jesus Christ.

¹⁷ Indeed you bear the name of a Jew, rest on the law, glory in God, ¹⁸ know his will, and approve the things that are excellent, being instructed out of the law, ¹⁹ and are confident that you yourself are a guide of the blind, a light to those who are in darkness, ²⁰ a corrector of the foolish, a teacher of babies, having in the law the form of knowledge and of the truth. ²¹ You therefore who teach another, don't you teach yourself? You who preach that a man shouldn't steal, do you steal? ²² You who say a man shouldn't commit adultery, do you commit adultery? You who abhor idols, do you rob temples? ²³ You who glory in the law, do you dishonor God by disobeying the law?

24 For "the name of God is blasphemed among the Gentiles because of you," just as it is written. 25 For circumcision indeed profits, if you are a doer of the law, but if you are a transgressor of the law, your circumcision has become uncircumcision. 26 If therefore the uncircumcised keep the ordinances of the law, won't his uncircumcision be accounted as circumcision? 27 Won't the uncircumcision which is by nature, if it fulfills the law, judge you, who with the letter and circumcision are a transgressor of the law? 28 For he is not a Jew who is one outwardly, neither is that circumcision which is outward in the flesh; 29 but he is a Jew who is one inwardly, and circumcision is that of the heart, in the spirit not in the letter; whose praise is not from men, but from God.

He is a Jew who is one inwardly, and circumcision is that of the heart, in the spirit not in the letter; whose praise is not from men, but from God.

OBSERVATION:
What do you notice? Write your questions.

WHO? Who speaks or is spoken to? Who is present or mentioned?

_____
_____
_____
_____
_____
_____

WHAT? What action or dialogue has taken place? What questions does this bring up?

_____
_____
_____
_____
_____
_____
_____
_____

WHERE? Whose house? What city? What nation?

_____
_____
_____
_____
_____

WHEN? What time, what day, what week, after what, etc?

_____
_____
_____
_____
_____

WHY?
What led to the action or dialogue that took place in this passage? Record every question you have about the purpose for what is said or done.

OTHER QUESTIONS & OBSERVATIONS

CONTENT
Record figures of speech, questions and answers, lists, comparisons, etc. What questions do these bring up?

_____
_____
_____
_____
_____
_____
_____
_____
_____
_____

CONTEXT
What is the immediate context and the broader context? What happens right before and after this passage?

_____
_____
_____
_____
_____
_____

COMPARISON
Track down scripture quotations, compare similar passages, notice other uses in scripture of special terms, names, or ideas.

_____
_____
_____
_____
_____
_____
_____

CULTURE
How does the cultural context influence this passage? What questions do you need answered about the culture to understand it better?

CONSULTATION
Explore commentaries and sermons on this passage and record helpful thoughts.

APPLICATION
Keeping in mind the meaning of this passage in its original context, how can you apply this passage to your life?

3

Then what advantage does the Jew have? Or what is the profit of circumcision? ² Much in every way! Because first of all, they were entrusted with the revelations of God. ³ For what if some were without faith? Will their lack of faith nullify the faithfulness of God? ⁴ May it never be! Yes, let God be found true, but every man a liar. As it is written,

"that you might be justified in your words,
   and might prevail when you come into judgment."

⁵ But if our unrighteousness commends the righteousness of God, what will we say? Is God unrighteous who inflicts wrath? I speak like men do. ⁶ May it never be! For then how will God judge the world? ⁷ For if the truth of God through my lie abounded to his glory, why am I also still judged as a sinner? ⁸ Why not (as we are slanderously reported, and as some affirm that we say), "Let's do evil, that good may come?" Those who say so are justly condemned.

⁹ What then? Are we better than they? No, in no way. For we previously warned both Jews and Greeks that they are all under sin.

Yes, let God be found true, but every man a liar.

¹⁰ As it is written,

"There is no one righteous;
  no, not one.
¹¹ There is no one who understands.
  There is no one who seeks after God.
¹² They have all turned away.
  They have together become unprofitable.
There is no one who does good,
  no, not so much as one."
¹³ "Their throat is an open tomb.
  With their tongues they have used deceit."
"The poison of vipers is under their lips."
¹⁴   "Their mouth is full of cursing and bitterness."
¹⁵ "Their feet are swift to shed blood.
¹⁶   Destruction and misery are in their ways.
¹⁷   The way of peace, they haven't known."
¹⁸ "There is no fear of God before their eyes."

¹⁹ Now we know that whatever things the law says, it speaks to those who are under the law, that every mouth may be closed, and all the world may be brought under the judgment of God.

²⁰ Because by the works of the law, no flesh will be justified in his sight; for through the law comes the knowledge of sin. ²¹ But now apart from the law, a righteousness of God has been revealed, being testified by the law and the prophets; ²² even the righteousness of God through faith in Jesus Christ to all and on all those who believe. For there is no distinction, ²³ for all have sinned, and fall short of the glory of God; ²⁴ being justified freely by his grace through the redemption that is in Christ Jesus; ²⁵ whom God sent to be an atoning sacrifice, through faith in his blood, for a demonstration of his righteousness through the passing over of prior sins, in God's forbearance; ²⁶ to demonstrate his righteousness at this present time; that he might himself be just, and the justifier of him who has faith in Jesus.

²⁷ Where then is the boasting? It is excluded. By what kind of law? Of works? No, but by a law of faith. ²⁸ We maintain therefore that a man is justified by faith apart from the works of the law. ²⁹ Or is God the God of Jews only? Isn't he the God of Gentiles also? Yes, of Gentiles also, ³⁰ since indeed there is one God who will justify the circumcised by faith, and the uncircumcised through faith. ³¹ Do we then nullify the law through faith? May it never be! No, we establish the law.

WHY?
What led to the action or dialogue that took place in this passage? Record every question you have about the purpose for what is said or done.

OTHER QUESTIONS & OBSERVATIONS

CONTENT
Record figures of speech, questions and answers, lists, comparisons, etc. What questions do these bring up?

_____

CONTEXT
What is the immediate context and the broader context? What happens right before and after this passage?

_____

COMPARISON
Track down scripture quotations, compare similar passages, notice other uses in scripture of special terms, names, or ideas.

_____

CULTURE
How does the cultural context influence this passage? What questions do you need answered about the culture to understand it better?

_____
_____
_____
_____
_____
_____
_____
_____
_____
_____
_____

CONSULTATION
Explore commentaries and sermons on this passage and record helpful thoughts.

_____
_____
_____
_____
_____
_____
_____
_____
_____
_____
_____
_____
_____
_____

APPLICATION
Keeping in mind the meaning of this passage in its original context, how can you apply this passage to your life?

4

What then will we say that Abraham, our forefather, has found according to the flesh? ² For if Abraham was justified by works, he has something to boast about, but not toward God. ³ For what does the Scripture say? "Abraham believed God, and it was accounted to him for righteousness." ⁴ Now to him who works, the reward is not counted as grace, but as something owed. ⁵ But to him who doesn't work, but believes in him who justifies the ungodly, his faith is accounted for righteousness. ⁶ Even as David also pronounces blessing on the man to whom God counts righteousness apart from works,

⁷ "Blessed are they whose iniquities are forgiven,
   whose sins are covered.
⁸ Blessed is the man whom the Lord will by no means charge with sin."

⁹ Is this blessing then pronounced on the circumcised, or on the uncircumcised also? For we say that faith was accounted to Abraham for righteousness. ¹⁰ How then was it counted? When he was in circumcision, or in uncircumcision? Not in circumcision, but in uncircumcision.

Blessed are they whose iniquities are forgiven

¹¹ He received the sign of circumcision, a seal of the righteousness of the faith which he had while he was in uncircumcision, that he might be the father of all those who believe, though they might be in uncircumcision, that righteousness might also be accounted to them. ¹² He is the father of circumcision to those who not only are of the circumcision, but who also walk in the steps of that faith of our father Abraham, which he had in uncircumcision.

¹³ For the promise to Abraham and to his offspring that he should be heir of the world wasn't through the law, but through the righteousness of faith. ¹⁴ For if those who are of the law are heirs, faith is made void, and the promise is made of no effect. ¹⁵ For the law produces wrath, for where there is no law, neither is there disobedience. ¹⁶ For this cause it is of faith, that it may be according to grace, to the end that the promise may be sure to all the offspring, not to that only which is of the law, but to that also which is of the faith of Abraham, who is the father of us all.

¹⁷ As it is written, "I have made you a father of many nations." This is in the presence of him whom he believed: God, who gives life to the dead, and calls the things that are not, as though they were. ¹⁸ Besides hope, Abraham in hope believed, to the end that he might become a father of many nations, according to that which had been spoken, "So will your offspring be."

¹⁹ Without being weakened in faith, he didn't consider his own body, already having been worn out, (he being about a hundred years old), and the deadness of Sarah's womb. ²⁰ Yet, looking to the promise of God, he didn't waver through unbelief, but grew strong through faith, giving glory to God, ²¹ and being fully assured that what he had promised, he was also able to perform. ²² Therefore it also was "credited to him for righteousness." ²³ Now it was not written that it was accounted to him for his sake alone, ²⁴ but for our sake also, to whom it will be accounted, who believe in him who raised Jesus, our Lord, from the dead, ²⁵ who was delivered up for our trespasses, and was raised for our justification.

Yet, looking to the promise of God, he didn't waver through unbelief, but grew strong through faith, giving glory to God

OBSERVATION: What do you notice? Write your questions.

WHO?
Who speaks or is spoken to? Who is present or mentioned?

_____
_____
_____
_____
_____
_____

WHAT?
What action or dialogue has taken place? What questions does this bring up?

_____
_____
_____
_____
_____
_____
_____
_____

WHERE?
Whose house? What city? What nation?

_____
_____
_____
_____
_____

WHEN?
What time, what day, what week, after what, etc?

_____
_____
_____
_____
_____

WHY?
What led to the action or dialogue that took place in this passage? Record every question you have about the purpose for what is said or done.

OTHER QUESTIONS & OBSERVATIONS

CONTENT
Record figures of speech, questions and answers, lists, comparisons, etc. What questions do these bring up?

_____
_____
_____
_____
_____
_____
_____
_____
_____

CONTEXT
What is the immediate context and the broader context? What happens right before and after this passage?

_____
_____
_____
_____
_____
_____

COMPARISON
Track down scripture quotations, compare similar passages, notice other uses in scripture of special terms, names, or ideas.

_____
_____
_____
_____
_____
_____
_____

CULTURE
How does the cultural context influence this passage? What questions do you need answered about the culture to understand it better?

_____
_____
_____
_____
_____
_____
_____
_____
_____
_____
_____
_____

CONSULTATION
Explore commentaries and sermons on this passage and record helpful thoughts.

_____
_____
_____
_____
_____
_____
_____
_____
_____
_____
_____
_____
_____
_____
_____
_____

APPLICATION
Keeping in mind the meaning of this passage in its original context, how can you apply this passage to your life?

5 Being therefore justified by faith, we have peace with God through our Lord Jesus Christ; ² through whom we also have our access by faith into this grace in which we stand. We rejoice in hope of the glory of God. ³ Not only this, but we also rejoice in our sufferings, knowing that suffering produces perseverance; ⁴ and perseverance, proven character; and proven character, hope: ⁵ and hope doesn't disappoint us, because God's love has been poured into our hearts through the Holy Spirit who was given to us. ⁶ For while we were yet weak, at the right time Christ died for the ungodly. ⁷ For one will hardly die for a righteous man. Yet perhaps for a good person someone would even dare to die. ⁸ But God commends his own love toward us, in that while we were yet sinners, Christ died for us.

⁹ Much more then, being now justified by his blood, we will be saved from God's wrath through him. ¹⁰ For if while we were enemies, we were reconciled to God through the death of his Son, much more, being reconciled, we will be saved by his life.
¹¹ Not only so, but we also rejoice in God through our Lord Jesus Christ, through whom we have now received the reconciliation. ¹² Therefore as sin entered into the world through one man, and death through sin; so death passed to all men, because all sinned.

¹³ For until the law, sin was in the world; but sin is not charged when there is no law. ¹⁴ Nevertheless death reigned from Adam until Moses, even over those whose sins weren't like Adam's disobedience, who is a foreshadowing of him who was to come. ¹⁵ But the free gift isn't like the trespass. For if by the trespass of the one the many died, much more did the grace of God, and the gift by the grace of the one man, Jesus Christ, abound to the many. ¹⁶ The gift is not as through one who sinned; for the judgment came by one to condemnation, but the free gift came of many trespasses to justification. ¹⁷ For if by the trespass of the one, death reigned through the one; so much more will those who receive the abundance of grace and of the gift of righteousness reign in life through the one, Jesus Christ.

¹⁸ So then as through one trespass, all men were condemned; even so through one act of righteousness, all men were justified to life. ¹⁹ For as through the one man's disobedience many were made sinners, even so through the obedience of the one, many will be made righteous. ²⁰ The law came in that the trespass might abound; but where sin abounded, grace abounded more exceedingly; ²¹ that as sin reigned in death, even so grace might reign through righteousness to eternal life through Jesus Christ our Lord.

WHY?
What led to the action or dialogue that took place in this passage? Record every question you have about the purpose for what is said or done.

OTHER QUESTIONS & OBSERVATIONS

CONTENT
Record figures of speech, questions and answers, lists, comparisons, etc. What questions do these bring up?

_____
_____
_____
_____
_____
_____
_____
_____
_____

CONTEXT
What is the immediate context and the broader context? What happens right before and after this passage?

_____
_____
_____
_____
_____
_____

COMPARISON
Track down scripture quotations, compare similar passages, notice other uses in scripture of special terms, names, or ideas.

_____
_____
_____
_____
_____
_____

CULTURE
How does the cultural context influence this passage? What questions do you need answered about the culture to understand it better?

_____
_____
_____
_____
_____
_____
_____
_____
_____
_____
_____
_____

CONSULTATION
Explore commentaries and sermons on this passage and record helpful thoughts.

_____
_____
_____
_____
_____
_____
_____
_____
_____
_____
_____
_____
_____
_____
_____
_____

APPLICATION
Keeping in mind the meaning of this passage in its original context, how can you apply this passage to your life?

6 What shall we say then? Shall we continue in sin, that grace may abound? ² May it never be! We who died to sin, how could we live in it any longer? ³ Or don't you know that all we who were baptized into Christ Jesus were baptized into his death? ⁴ We were buried therefore with him through baptism into death, that just as Christ was raised from the dead through the glory of the Father, so we also might walk in newness of life. ⁵ For if we have become united with him in the likeness of his death, we will also be part of his resurrection; ⁶ knowing this, that our old man was crucified with him, that the body of sin might be done away with, so that we would no longer be in bondage to sin. ⁷ For he who has died has been freed from sin. ⁸ But if we died with Christ, we believe that we will also live with him; ⁹ knowing that Christ, being raised from the dead, dies no more. Death no longer has dominion over him! ¹⁰ For the death that he died, he died to sin one time; but the life that he lives, he lives to God. ¹¹ Thus consider yourselves also to be dead to sin, but alive to God in Christ Jesus our Lord.

¹² Therefore don't let sin reign in your mortal body, that you should obey it in its lusts. ¹³ Also, do not present your members to sin as instruments of unrighteousness, but present yourselves to God as alive from the dead, and your members as instruments of righteousness to God. ¹⁴ For sin will not have dominion over you. For you are not under law, but under grace.

¹⁵ What then? Shall we sin, because we are not under law, but under grace? May it never be! ¹⁶ Don't you know that when you present yourselves as servants and obey someone, you are the servants of whomever you obey; whether of sin to death, or of obedience to righteousness? ¹⁷ But thanks be to God, that, whereas you were bondservants of sin, you became obedient from the heart to that form of teaching to which you were delivered.
¹⁸ Being made free from sin, you became bondservants of righteousness.

¹⁹ I speak in human terms because of the weakness of your flesh, for as you presented your members as servants to uncleanness and to wickedness upon wickedness, even so now present your members as servants to righteousness for sanctification. ²⁰ For when you were servants of sin, you were free from righteousness. ²¹ What fruit then did you have at that time in the things of which you are now ashamed? For the end of those things is death. ²² But now, being made free from sin and having become servants of God, you have your fruit of sanctification and the result of eternal life.

²³ For the wages of sin is death, but the free gift of God is eternal life in Christ Jesus our Lord.

OBSERVATION:
What do you notice? Write your questions.

WHO?
Who speaks or is spoken to? Who is present or mentioned?

_____
_____
_____
_____
_____
_____

WHAT?
What action or dialogue has taken place? What questions does this bring up?

_____
_____
_____
_____
_____
_____
_____
_____

WHERE?
Whose house? What city? What nation?

_____
_____
_____
_____
_____

WHEN?
What time, what day, what week, after what, etc?

_____
_____
_____
_____
_____

WHY?
What led to the action or dialogue that took place in this passage? Record every question you have about the purpose for what is said or done.

OTHER QUESTIONS & OBSERVATIONS

CONTENT
Record figures of speech, questions and answers, lists, comparisons, etc. What questions do these bring up?

_____
_____
_____
_____
_____
_____
_____
_____
_____
_____

CONTEXT
What is the immediate context and the broader context? What happens right before and after this passage?

_____
_____
_____
_____
_____
_____

COMPARISON
Track down scripture quotations, compare similar passages, notice other uses in scripture of special terms, names, or ideas.

_____
_____
_____
_____
_____
_____
_____

CULTURE
How does the cultural context influence this passage? What questions do you need answered about the culture to understand it better?

CONSULTATION
Explore commentaries and sermons on this passage and record helpful thoughts.

APPLICATION
Keeping in mind the meaning of this passage in its original context, how can you apply this passage to your life?

7 Or don't you know, brothers (for I speak to men who know the law), that the law has dominion over a man for as long as he lives? ² For the woman that has a husband is bound by law to the husband while he lives, but if the husband dies, she is discharged from the law of the husband. ³ So then if, while the husband lives, she is joined to another man, she would be called an adulteress. But if the husband dies, she is free from the law, so that she is no adulteress, though she is joined to another man.
⁴ Therefore, my brothers, you also were made dead to the law through the body of Christ, that you would be joined to another, to him who was raised from the dead, that we might produce fruit to God. ⁵ For when we were in the flesh, the sinful passions which were through the law worked in our members to bring out fruit to death. ⁶ But now we have been discharged from the law, having died to that in which we were held; so that we serve in newness of the spirit, and not in oldness of the letter.

⁷ What shall we say then? Is the law sin? May it never be! However, I wouldn't have known sin, except through the law. For I wouldn't have known coveting, unless the law had said, "You shall not covet." ⁸ But sin, finding occasion through the commandment, produced in me all kinds of coveting. For apart from the law, sin is dead.

⁹ I was alive apart from the law once, but when the commandment came, sin revived, and I died. ¹⁰ The commandment which was for life, this I found to be for death; ¹¹ for sin, finding occasion through the commandment, deceived me, and through it killed me.

¹² Therefore the law indeed is holy, and the commandment holy, and righteous, and good.

¹³ Did then that which is good become death to me? May it never be! But sin, that it might be shown to be sin, was producing death in me through that which is good; that through the commandment sin might become exceedingly sinful. ¹⁴ For we know that the law is spiritual, but I am fleshly, sold under sin. ¹⁵ For I don't know what I am doing. For I don't practice what I desire to do; but what I hate, that I do. ¹⁶ But if what I don't desire, that I do, I consent to the law that it is good. ¹⁷ So now it is no more I that do it, but sin which dwells in me. ¹⁸ For I know that in me, that is, in my flesh, dwells no good thing. For desire is present with me, but I don't find it doing that which is good. ¹⁹ For the good which I desire, I don't do; but the evil which I don't desire, that I practice. ²⁰ But if what I don't desire, that I do, it is no more I that do it, but sin which dwells in me.

²¹ I find then the law that, to me, while I desire to do good, evil is present. ²² For I delight in God's law after the inward person, ²³ but I see a different law in my members, warring against the law of my mind, and bringing me into captivity under the law of sin which is in my members. ²⁴ What a wretched man I am! Who will deliver me out of the body of this death? ²⁵ I thank God through Jesus Christ, our Lord! So then with the mind, I myself serve God's law, but with the flesh, sin's law.

What I wretched man I am! Who will deliver me out of the body of this death? I thank God through Jesus Christ, our Lord!

WHY? What led to the action or dialogue that took place in this passage?
Record every question you have about the purpose for what is said or done.

OTHER QUESTIONS & OBSERVATIONS

CONTENT
Record figures of speech, questions and answers, lists, comparisons, etc. What questions do these bring up?

_____
_____
_____
_____
_____
_____
_____
_____
_____

CONTEXT
What is the immediate context and the broader context? What happens right before and after this passage?

_____
_____
_____
_____
_____

COMPARISON
Track down scripture quotations, compare similar passages, notice other uses in scripture of special terms, names, or ideas.

_____
_____
_____
_____
_____
_____

CULTURE
How does the cultural context influence this passage? What questions do you need answered about the culture to understand it better?

_____
_____
_____
_____
_____
_____
_____
_____
_____
_____
_____

CONSULTATION
Explore commentaries and sermons on this passage and record helpful thoughts.

_____
_____
_____
_____
_____
_____
_____
_____
_____
_____
_____
_____
_____
_____

APPLICATION

Keeping in mind the meaning of this passage in its original context, how can you apply this passage to your life?

8 There is therefore now no condemnation to those who are in Christ Jesus, who don't walk according to the flesh, but according to the Spirit. ² For the law of the Spirit of life in Christ Jesus made me free from the law of sin and of death. ³ For what the law couldn't do, in that it was weak through the flesh, God did, sending his own Son in the likeness of sinful flesh and for sin, he condemned sin in the flesh; ⁴ that the ordinance of the law might be fulfilled in us, who walk not after the flesh, but after the Spirit. ⁵ For those who live according to the flesh set their minds on the things of the flesh, but those who live according to the Spirit, the things of the Spirit. ⁶ For the mind of the flesh is death, but the mind of the Spirit is life and peace; ⁷ because the mind of the flesh is hostile toward God; for it is not subject to God's law, neither indeed can it be.

⁸ Those who are in the flesh can't please God. ⁹ But you are not in the flesh but in the Spirit, if it is so that the Spirit of God dwells in you. But if any man doesn't have the Spirit of Christ, he is not his. ¹⁰ If Christ is in you, the body is dead because of sin, but the spirit is alive because of righteousness. ¹¹ But if the Spirit of him who raised up Jesus from the dead dwells in you, he who raised up Christ Jesus from the dead will also give life to your mortal bodies through his Spirit who dwells in you.

¹² So then, brothers, we are debtors, not to the flesh, to live after the flesh. ¹³ For if you live after the flesh, you must die; but if by the Spirit you put to death the deeds of the body, you will live. ¹⁴ For as many as are led by the Spirit of God, these are children of God. ¹⁵ For you didn't receive the spirit of bondage again to fear, but you received the Spirit of adoption, by whom we cry, "Abba! Father!"

¹⁶ The Spirit himself testifies with our spirit that we are children of God; ¹⁷ and if children, then heirs: heirs of God and joint heirs with Christ, if indeed we suffer with him, that we may also be glorified with him.

¹⁸ For I consider that the sufferings of this present time are not worthy to be compared with the glory which will be revealed toward us. ¹⁹ For the creation waits with eager expectation for the children of God to be revealed. ²⁰ For the creation was subjected to vanity, not of its own will, but because of him who subjected it, in hope ²¹ that the creation itself also will be delivered from the bondage of decay into the liberty of the glory of the children of God.

For as many as are led by the Spirit of God, these are children of God.

²² For we know that the whole creation groans and travails in pain together until now. ²³ Not only so, but ourselves also, who have the first fruits of the Spirit, even we ourselves groan within ourselves, waiting for adoption, the redemption of our body. ²⁴ For we were saved in hope, but hope that is seen is not hope. For who hopes for that which he sees? ²⁵ But if we hope for that which we don't see, we wait for it with patience.

²⁶ In the same way, the Spirit also helps our weaknesses, for we don't know how to pray as we ought. But the Spirit himself makes intercession for us with groanings which can't be uttered. ²⁷ He who searches the hearts knows what is on the Spirit's mind, because he makes intercession for the saints according to God.

²⁸ We know that all things work together for good for those who love God, for those who are called according to his purpose. ²⁹ For whom he foreknew, he also predestined to be conformed to the image of his Son, that he might be the firstborn among many brothers. ³⁰ Whom he predestined, those he also called. Whom he called, those he also justified. Whom he justified, those he also glorified.

³¹ What then shall we say about these things? If God is for us, who can be against us? ³² He who didn't spare his own Son, but delivered him up for us all, how would he not also with him freely give us all things? ³³ Who could bring a charge against God's chosen ones? It is God who justifies. ³⁴ Who is he who condemns? It is Christ who died, yes rather, who was raised from the dead, who is at the right hand of God, who also makes intercession for us.

³⁵ Who shall separate us from the love of Christ? Could oppression, or anguish, or persecution, or famine, or nakedness, or peril, or sword? ³⁶ Even as it is written, "For your sake we are killed all day long.
We were accounted as sheep for the slaughter."

³⁷ No, in all these things, we are more than conquerors through him who loved us. ³⁸ For I am persuaded that neither death, nor life, nor angels, nor principalities, nor things present, nor things to come, nor powers, ³⁹ nor height, nor depth, nor any other created thing will be able to separate us from God's love which is in Christ Jesus our Lord.

If God is for us, who can be against us?

WHY?
What led to the action or dialogue that took place in this passage? Record every question you have about the purpose for what is said or done.

OTHER QUESTIONS & OBSERVATIONS

CONTENT
Record figures of speech, questions and answers, lists, comparisons, etc. What questions do these bring up?

_____
_____
_____
_____
_____
_____
_____
_____
_____

CONTEXT
What is the immediate context and the broader context? What happens right before and after this passage?

_____
_____
_____
_____
_____
_____

COMPARISON
Track down scripture quotations, compare similar passages, notice other uses in scripture of special terms, names, or ideas.

_____
_____
_____
_____
_____
_____

CULTURE
How does the cultural context influence this passage? What questions do you need answered about the culture to understand it better?

CONSULTATION
Explore commentaries and sermons on this passage and record helpful thoughts.

APPLICATION
Keeping in mind the meaning of this passage in its original context, how can you apply this passage to your life?

9 I tell the truth in Christ. I am not lying, my conscience testifying with me in the Holy Spirit ² that I have great sorrow and unceasing pain in my heart. ³ For I could wish that I myself were accursed from Christ for my brothers' sake, my relatives according to the flesh ⁴ who are Israelites; whose is the adoption, the glory, the covenants, the giving of the law, the service, and the promises; ⁵ of whom are the fathers, and from whom is Christ as concerning the flesh, who is over all, God, blessed forever. Amen.

⁶ But it is not as though the word of God has come to nothing. For they are not all Israel that are of Israel. ⁷ Neither, because they are Abraham's offspring, are they all children. But, "your offspring will be accounted as from Isaac." ⁸ That is, it is not the children of the flesh who are children of God, but the children of the promise are counted as heirs. ⁹ For this is a word of promise, "At the appointed time I will come, and Sarah will have a son." ¹⁰ Not only so, but Rebekah also conceived by one, by our father Isaac. ¹¹ For being not yet born, neither having done anything good or bad, that the purpose of God according to election might stand, not of works, but of him who calls, ¹² it was said to her, "The elder will serve the younger." ¹³ Even as it is written, "Jacob I loved, but Esau I hated."

¹⁴ What shall we say then? Is there unrighteousness with God? May it never be! ¹⁵ For he said to Moses, "I will have mercy on whom I have mercy, and I will have compassion on whom I have compassion." ¹⁶ So then it is not of him who wills, nor of him who runs, but of God who has mercy. ¹⁷ For the Scripture says to Pharaoh, "For this very purpose I caused you to be raised up, that I might show in you my power, and that my name might be proclaimed in all the earth." ¹⁸ So then, he has mercy on whom he desires, and he hardens whom he desires.

¹⁹ You will say then to me, "Why does he still find fault? For who withstands his will?" ²⁰ But indeed, O man, who are you to reply against God? Will the thing formed ask him who formed it, "Why did you make me like this?" ²¹ Or hasn't the potter a right over the clay, from the same lump to make one part a vessel for honor, and another for dishonor? ²² What if God, willing to show his wrath and to make his power known, endured with much patience vessels of wrath prepared for destruction, ²³ and that he might make known the riches of his glory on vessels of mercy, which he prepared beforehand for glory, ²⁴ us, whom he also called, not from the Jews only, but also from the Gentiles?

25 As he says also in Hosea,

"I will call them 'my people,' which were not my people;
   and her 'beloved,' who was not beloved."

26 "It will be that in the place where it was said to them,
'You are not my people,'
   there they will be called 'children of the living God.'"

27 Isaiah cries concerning Israel,

"If the number of the children of Israel are as the sand of the sea,
   it is the remnant who will be saved;

28 for He will finish the work and cut it short in righteousness,
   because the LORD will make a short work upon the earth."

29 As Isaiah has said before,

"Unless the Lord of Armies had left us a seed,
   we would have become like Sodom,
   and would have been made like Gomorrah."

30 What shall we say then? That the Gentiles, who didn't follow after righteousness, attained to righteousness, even the righteousness which is of faith; 31 but Israel, following after a law of righteousness, didn't arrive at the law of righteousness. 32 Why? Because they didn't seek it by faith, but as it were by works of the law. They stumbled over the stumbling stone; 33 even as it is written,

"Behold, I lay in Zion a stumbling stone and a rock of offense; and no one who believes in him will be disappointed."

WHY? What led to the action or dialogue that took place in this passage?
Record every question you have about the purpose for what is said or done.

_____
_____
_____
_____
_____
_____
_____
_____
_____
_____
_____
_____
_____

OTHER QUESTIONS & OBSERVATIONS

_____
_____
_____
_____
_____
_____
_____
_____
_____
_____
_____
_____
_____
_____

CONTENT
Record figures of speech, questions and answers, lists, comparisons, etc. What questions do these bring up?

CONTEXT
What is the immediate context and the broader context? What happens right before and after this passage?

COMPARISON
Track down scripture quotations, compare similar passages, notice other uses in scripture of special terms, names, or ideas.

CULTURE
How does the cultural context influence this passage? What questions do you need answered about the culture to understand it better?

CONSULTATION
Explore commentaries and sermons on this passage and record helpful thoughts.

APPLICATION
Keeping in mind the meaning of this passage in its original context, how can you apply this passage to your life?

10 Brothers, my heart's desire and my prayer to God is for Israel, that they may be saved. ² For I testify about them that they have a zeal for God, but not according to knowledge. ³ For being ignorant of God's righteousness, and seeking to establish their own righteousness, they didn't subject themselves to the righteousness of God. ⁴ For Christ is the fulfillment of the law for righteousness to everyone who believes. ⁵ For Moses writes about the righteousness of the law, "The one who does them will live by them." ⁶ But the righteousness which is of faith says this, "Don't say in your heart, 'Who will ascend into heaven?' (that is, to bring Christ down); ⁷ or, 'Who will descend into the abyss?' (that is, to bring Christ up from the dead.)" ⁸ But what does it say? "The word is near you, in your mouth, and in your heart;" that is, the word of faith which we preach: ⁹ that if you will confess with your mouth that Jesus is Lord, and believe in your heart that God raised him from the dead, you will be saved. ¹⁰ For with the heart, one believes resulting in righteousness; and with the mouth confession is made resulting in salvation. ¹¹ For the Scripture says, "Whoever believes in him will not be disappointed."

¹² For there is no distinction between Jew and Greek; for the same Lord is Lord of all, and is rich to all who call on him.

¹³ For, "Whoever will call on the name of the Lord will be saved." ¹⁴ How then will they call on him in whom they have not believed? How will they believe in him whom they have not heard? How will they hear without a preacher? ¹⁵ And how will they preach unless they are sent? As it is written:

"How beautiful are the feet of those who preach the Good News of peace,

    who bring glad tidings of good things!"

¹⁶ But they didn't all listen to the glad news. For Isaiah says, "Lord, who has believed our report?" ¹⁷ So faith comes by hearing, and hearing by the word of God.

¹⁸ But I say, didn't they hear? Yes, most certainly,

"Their sound went out into all the earth,

    their words to the ends of the world."

¹⁹ But I ask, didn't Israel know? First Moses says,

"I will provoke you to jealousy with that which is no nation.

    I will make you angry with a nation void of understanding."

²⁰ Isaiah is very bold and says,

"I was found by those who didn't seek me.

    I was revealed to those who didn't ask for me."

²¹ But about Israel he says, "All day long I stretched out my hands to a disobedient and contrary people."

WHY?
What led to the action or dialogue that took place in this passage? Record every question you have about the purpose for what is said or done.

OTHER QUESTIONS & OBSERVATIONS

CONTENT
Record figures of speech, questions and answers, lists, comparisons, etc. What questions do these bring up?

_____
_____
_____
_____
_____
_____
_____
_____

CONTEXT
What is the immediate context and the broader context? What happens right before and after this passage?

_____
_____
_____
_____
_____
_____

COMPARISON
Track down scripture quotations, compare similar passages, notice other uses in scripture of special terms, names, or ideas.

_____
_____
_____
_____
_____
_____

CULTURE
How does the cultural context influence this passage? What questions do you need answered about the culture to understand it better?

CONSULTATION
Explore commentaries and sermons on this passage and record helpful thoughts.

APPLICATION
Keeping in mind the meaning of this passage in its original context, how can you apply this passage to your life?

11 I ask then, did God reject his people? May it never be! For I also am an Israelite, a descendant of Abraham, of the tribe of Benjamin. ² God didn't reject his people, which he foreknew. Or don't you know what the Scripture says about Elijah? How he pleads with God against Israel: ³ "Lord, they have killed your prophets, they have broken down your altars. I am left alone, and they seek my life." ⁴ But how does God answer him? "I have reserved for myself seven thousand men who have not bowed the knee to Baal." ⁵ Even so then at this present time also there is a remnant according to the election of grace. ⁶ And if by grace, then it is no longer of works; otherwise grace is no longer grace. But if it is of works, it is no longer grace; otherwise work is no longer work.

⁷ What then? That which Israel seeks for, that he didn't obtain, but the chosen ones obtained it, and the rest were hardened. ⁸ According as it is written, "God gave them a spirit of stupor, eyes that they should not see, and ears that they should not hear, to this very day."

⁹ David says,
"Let their table be made a snare, a trap,
   a stumbling block, and a retribution to them.
¹⁰ Let their eyes be darkened, that they may not see.
   Always keep their backs bent."

[11] I ask then, did they stumble that they might fall? May it never be! But by their fall salvation has come to the Gentiles, to provoke them to jealousy. [12] Now if their fall is the riches of the world, and their loss the riches of the Gentiles; how much more their fullness? [13] For I speak to you who are Gentiles. Since then as I am an apostle to Gentiles, I glorify my ministry; [14] if by any means I may provoke to jealousy those who are my flesh, and may save some of them. [15] For if the rejection of them is the reconciling of the world, what would their acceptance be, but life from the dead? [16] If the first fruit is holy, so is the lump. If the root is holy, so are the branches.

[17] But if some of the branches were broken off, and you, being a wild olive, were grafted in among them and became partaker with them of the root and of the richness of the olive tree, [18] don't boast over the branches. But if you boast, it is not you who support the root, but the root supports you. [19] You will say then, "Branches were broken off, that I might be grafted in." [20] True; by their unbelief they were broken off, and you stand by your faith. Don't be conceited, but fear; [21] for if God didn't spare the natural branches, neither will he spare you. [22] See then the goodness and severity of God. Toward those who fell, severity; but toward you, goodness, if you continue in his goodness; otherwise you also will be cut off. [23] They also, if they don't continue in their unbelief, will be grafted in, for God is able to graft them in again.

²⁴ For if you were cut out of that which is by nature a wild olive tree, and were grafted contrary to nature into a good olive tree, how much more will these, which are the natural branches, be grafted into their own olive tree?

²⁵ For I don't desire you to be ignorant, brothers, of this mystery, so that you won't be wise in your own conceits, that a partial hardening has happened to Israel, until the fullness of the Gentiles has come in, ²⁶ and so all Israel will be saved. Even as it is written,
"There will come out of Zion the Deliverer,
  and he will turn away ungodliness from Jacob.
²⁷ This is my covenant with them,
  when I will take away their sins."

²⁸ Concerning the Good News, they are enemies for your sake. But concerning the election, they are beloved for the fathers' sake. ²⁹ For the gifts and the calling of God are irrevocable. ³⁰ For as you in time past were disobedient to God, but now have obtained mercy by their disobedience, ³¹ even so these also have now been disobedient, that by the mercy shown to you they may also obtain mercy. ³² For God has bound all to disobedience, that he might have mercy on all.

³³ Oh the depth of the riches both of the wisdom and the knowledge of God! How unsearchable are his judgments, and his ways past tracing out!

³⁴ "For who has known the mind of the Lord?
    Or who has been his counselor?"
³⁵ "Or who has first given to him,
    and it will be repaid to him again?"

³⁶ For of him, and through him, and to him are all things. To him be the glory for ever! Amen.

Oh the depth of the riches both of the wisdom and the knowledge of God! How unsearchable are his judgments, and his ways past tracing out!

WHY?
What led to the action or dialogue that took place in this passage? Record every question you have about the purpose for what is said or done.

_____
_____
_____
_____
_____
_____
_____
_____
_____
_____
_____
_____
_____

OTHER QUESTIONS & OBSERVATIONS

_____
_____
_____
_____
_____
_____
_____
_____
_____
_____
_____
_____
_____
_____

CONTENT
Record figures of speech, questions and answers, lists, comparisons, etc. What questions do these bring up?

_____
_____
_____
_____
_____
_____
_____
_____
_____

CONTEXT
What is the immediate context and the broader context? What happens right before and after this passage?

_____
_____
_____
_____
_____
_____

COMPARISON
Track down scripture quotations, compare similar passages, notice other uses in scripture of special terms, names, or ideas.

_____
_____
_____
_____
_____
_____
_____

CULTURE
How does the cultural context influence this passage? What questions do you need answered about the culture to understand it better?

CONSULTATION
Explore commentaries and sermons on this passage and record helpful thoughts.

APPLICATION
Keeping in mind the meaning of this passage in its original context, how can you apply this passage to your life?

12

Therefore I urge you, brothers, by the mercies of God, to present your bodies a living sacrifice, holy, acceptable to God, which is your spiritual service. ² Don't be conformed to this world, but be transformed by the renewing of your mind, so that you may prove what is the good, well-pleasing, and perfect will of God.

³ For I say through the grace that was given me, to every man who is among you, not to think of himself more highly than he ought to think; but to think reasonably, as God has apportioned to each person a measure of faith.

⁴ For even as we have many members in one body, and all the members don't have the same function, ⁵ so we, who are many, are one body in Christ, and individually members of one another, ⁶ having gifts differing according to the grace that was given to us: if prophecy, let's prophesy according to the proportion of our faith; ⁷ or service, let's give ourselves to service; or he who teaches, to his teaching; ⁸ or he who exhorts, to his exhorting; he who gives, let him do it with generosity; he who rules, with diligence; he who shows mercy, with cheerfulness.

Be transformed by the renewing of your mind

⁹ Let love be without hypocrisy. Abhor that which is evil. Cling to that which is good. ¹⁰ In love of the brothers be tenderly affectionate to one another; in honor preferring one another; ¹¹ not lagging in diligence; fervent in spirit; serving the Lord; ¹² rejoicing in hope; enduring in troubles; continuing steadfastly in prayer; ¹³ contributing to the needs of the saints; given to hospitality. ¹⁴ Bless those who persecute you; bless, and don't curse. ¹⁵ Rejoice with those who rejoice. Weep with those who weep. ¹⁶ Be of the same mind one toward another. Don't set your mind on high things, but associate with the humble. Don't be wise in your own conceits. ¹⁷ Repay no one evil for evil. Respect what is honorable in the sight of all men. ¹⁸ If it is possible, as much as it is up to you, be at peace with all men. ¹⁹ Don't seek revenge yourselves, beloved, but give place to God's wrath. For it is written, "Vengeance belongs to me; I will repay, says the Lord."

²⁰ Therefore
"If your enemy is hungry, feed him.
   If he is thirsty, give him a drink;
   for in doing so, you will heap coals of fire on his head."
²¹ Don't be overcome by evil, but overcome evil with good.

Overcome evil with good

WHY?
What led to the action or dialogue that took place in this passage? Record every question you have about the purpose for what is said or done.

OTHER QUESTIONS & OBSERVATIONS

CONTENT
Record figures of speech, questions and answers, lists, comparisons, etc. What questions do these bring up?

_____
_____
_____
_____
_____
_____
_____
_____
_____

CONTEXT
What is the immediate context and the broader context? What happens right before and after this passage?

_____
_____
_____
_____
_____
_____

COMPARISON
Track down scripture quotations, compare similar passages, notice other uses in scripture of special terms, names, or ideas.

_____
_____
_____
_____
_____
_____

CULTURE
How does the cultural context influence this passage? What questions do you need answered about the culture to understand it better?

CONSULTATION
Explore commentaries and sermons on this passage and record helpful thoughts.

APPLICATION
Keeping in mind the meaning of this passage in its original context, how can you apply this passage to your life?

13 Let every soul be in subjection to the higher authorities, for there is no authority except from God, and those who exist are ordained by God. ² Therefore he who resists the authority withstands the ordinance of God; and those who withstand will receive to themselves judgment. ³ For rulers are not a terror to the good work, but to the evil. Do you desire to have no fear of the authority? Do that which is good, and you will have praise from the authority, ⁴ for he is a servant of God to you for good. But if you do that which is evil, be afraid, for he doesn't bear the sword in vain; for he is a servant of God, an avenger for wrath to him who does evil. ⁵ Therefore you need to be in subjection, not only because of the wrath, but also for conscience' sake. ⁶ For this reason you also pay taxes, for they are servants of God's service, continually doing this very thing. ⁷ Therefore give everyone what you owe: if you owe taxes, pay taxes; if customs, then customs; if respect, then respect; if honor, then honor.

⁸ Owe no one anything, except to love one another; for he who loves his neighbor has fulfilled the law. ⁹ For the commandments, "You shall not commit adultery," "You shall not murder," "You shall not steal," "You shall not covet," and whatever other commandments there are, are all summed up in this saying, namely, "You shall love your neighbor as yourself." ¹⁰ Love doesn't harm a neighbor. Love therefore is the fulfillment of the law.

¹¹ Do this, knowing the time, that it is already time for you to awaken out of sleep, for salvation is now nearer to us than when we first believed. ¹² The night is far gone, and the day is near. Let's therefore throw off the deeds of darkness, and let's put on the armor of light. ¹³ Let's walk properly, as in the day; not in reveling and drunkenness, not in sexual promiscuity and lustful acts, and not in strife and jealousy. ¹⁴ But put on the Lord Jesus Christ, and make no provision for the flesh, for its lusts.

Salvation is now nearer to us than when we first believed.

OBSERVATION:
What do you notice? Write your questions.

WHO?
Who speaks or is spoken to? Who is present or mentioned?

_____
_____
_____
_____
_____
_____

WHAT?
What action or dialogue has taken place? What questions does this bring up?

_____
_____
_____
_____
_____
_____
_____
_____

WHERE?
Whose house? What city? What nation?

_____
_____
_____
_____
_____

WHEN?
What time, what day, what week, after what, etc?

_____
_____
_____
_____
_____

WHY?
What led to the action or dialogue that took place in this passage? Record every question you have about the purpose for what is said or done.

OTHER QUESTIONS & OBSERVATIONS

CONTENT
Record figures of speech, questions and answers, lists, comparisons, etc. What questions do these bring up?

CONTEXT
What is the immediate context and the broader context? What happens right before and after this passage?

COMPARISON
Track down scripture quotations, compare similar passages, notice other uses in scripture of special terms, names, or ideas.

CULTURE
How does the cultural context influence this passage? What questions do you need answered about the culture to understand it better?

CONSULTATION
Explore commentaries and sermons on this passage and record helpful thoughts.

APPLICATION
Keeping in mind the meaning of this passage in its original context, how can you apply this passage to your life?

14 Now accept one who is weak in faith, but not for disputes over opinions. ² One man has faith to eat all things, but he who is weak eats only vegetables. ³ Don't let him who eats despise him who doesn't eat. Don't let him who doesn't eat judge him who eats, for God has accepted him. ⁴ Who are you who judge another's servant? To his own lord he stands or falls. Yes, he will be made to stand, for God has power to make him stand.

⁵ One man esteems one day as more important. Another esteems every day alike. Let each man be fully assured in his own mind. ⁶ He who observes the day, observes it to the Lord; and he who does not observe the day, to the Lord he does not observe it. He who eats, eats to the Lord, for he gives God thanks. He who doesn't eat, to the Lord he doesn't eat, and gives God thanks. ⁷ For none of us lives to himself, and none dies to himself. ⁸ For if we live, we live to the Lord. Or if we die, we die to the Lord. If therefore we live or die, we are the Lord's. ⁹ For to this end Christ died, rose, and lived again, that he might be Lord of both the dead and the living.

¹⁰ But you, why do you judge your brother? Or you again, why do you despise your brother? For we will all stand before the judgment seat of Christ. ¹¹ For it is written,
"'As I live,' says the Lord, 'to me every knee will bow.
　Every tongue will confess to God.'"

¹² So then each one of us will give account of himself to God.

¹³ Therefore let's not judge one another any more, but judge this rather, that no man put a stumbling block in his brother's way, or an occasion for falling. ¹⁴ I know, and am persuaded in the Lord Jesus, that nothing is unclean of itself; except that to him who considers anything to be unclean, to him it is unclean. ¹⁵ Yet if because of food your brother is grieved, you walk no longer in love. Don't destroy with your food him for whom Christ died. ¹⁶ Then don't let your good be slandered, ¹⁷ for God's Kingdom is not eating and drinking, but righteousness, peace, and joy in the Holy Spirit. ¹⁸ For he who serves Christ in these things is acceptable to God and approved by men. ¹⁹ So then, let's follow after things which make for peace, and things by which we may build one another up. ²⁰ Don't overthrow God's work for food's sake. All things indeed are clean, however it is evil for that man who creates a stumbling block by eating. ²¹ It is good to not eat meat, drink wine, nor do anything by which your brother stumbles, is offended, or is made weak.

Don't destroy with your food him for whom Christ died.

²² Do you have faith? Have it to yourself before God. Happy is he who doesn't judge himself in that which he approves. ²³ But he who doubts is condemned if he eats, because it isn't of faith; and whatever is not of faith is sin. ²⁴ Now to him who is able to establish you according to my Good News and the preaching of Jesus Christ, according to the revelation of the mystery which has been kept secret through long ages, ²⁵ but now is revealed, and by the Scriptures of the prophets, according to the commandment of the eternal God, is made known for obedience of faith to all the nations; ²⁶ to the only wise God, through Jesus Christ, to whom be the glory forever! Amen.

Happy is he who doesn't judge himself in that which he approves.

OBSERVATION:
What do you notice? Write your questions.

WHO?
Who speaks or is spoken to? Who is present or mentioned?

_____
_____
_____
_____
_____
_____

WHAT?
What action or dialogue has taken place? What questions does this bring up?

_____
_____
_____
_____
_____
_____
_____
_____

WHERE?
Whose house? What city? What nation?

_____
_____
_____
_____
_____

WHEN?
What time, what day, what week, after what, etc?

_____
_____
_____
_____
_____

WHY?
What led to the action or dialogue that took place in this passage? Record every question you have about the purpose for what is said or done.

OTHER QUESTIONS & OBSERVATIONS

CONTENT
Record figures of speech, questions and answers, lists, comparisons, etc. What questions do these bring up?

_____
_____
_____
_____
_____
_____
_____
_____
_____

CONTEXT
What is the immediate context and the broader context? What happens right before and after this passage?

_____
_____
_____
_____
_____
_____

COMPARISON
Track down scripture quotations, compare similar passages, notice other uses in scripture of special terms, names, or ideas.

_____
_____
_____
_____
_____
_____
_____

CULTURE
How does the cultural context influence this passage? What questions do you need answered about the culture to understand it better?

_____

CONSULTATION
Explore commentaries and sermons on this passage and record helpful thoughts.

_____

APPLICATION

Keeping in mind the meaning of this passage in its original context, how can you apply this passage to your life?

15 Now we who are strong ought to bear the weaknesses of the weak, and not to please ourselves. ² Let each one of us please his neighbor for that which is good, to be building him up. ³ For even Christ didn't please himself. But, as it is written, "The reproaches of those who reproached you fell on me." ⁴ For whatever things were written before were written for our learning, that through perseverance and through encouragement of the Scriptures we might have hope. ⁵ Now the God of perseverance and of encouragement grant you to be of the same mind with one another according to Christ Jesus, ⁶ that with one accord you may with one mouth glorify the God and Father of our Lord Jesus Christ.

⁷ Therefore accept one another, even as Christ also accepted you, to the glory of God. ⁸ Now I say that Christ has been made a servant of the circumcision for the truth of God, that he might confirm the promises given to the fathers, ⁹ and that the Gentiles might glorify God for his mercy. As it is written,

"Therefore I will give praise to you among the Gentiles
   and sing to your name."

¹⁰ Again he says,
"Rejoice, you Gentiles, with his people." ¹¹ Again,
"Praise the Lord, all you Gentiles!
   Let all the peoples praise him."

¹² Again, Isaiah says,
"There will be the root of Jesse,
    he who arises to rule over the Gentiles;
    in him the Gentiles will hope."
¹³ Now may the God of hope fill you with all joy and peace in believing, that you may abound in hope, in the power of the Holy Spirit.
¹⁴ I myself am also persuaded about you, my brothers, that you yourselves are full of goodness, filled with all knowledge, able also to admonish others. ¹⁵ But I write the more boldly to you in part, as reminding you, because of the grace that was given to me by God, ¹⁶ that I should be a servant of Christ Jesus to the Gentiles, serving as a priest of the Good News of God, that the offering up of the Gentiles might be made acceptable, sanctified by the Holy Spirit. ¹⁷ I have therefore my boasting in Christ Jesus in things pertaining to God. ¹⁸ For I will not dare to speak of any things except those which Christ worked through me, for the obedience of the Gentiles, by word and deed, ¹⁹ in the power of signs and wonders, in the power of God's Spirit; so that from Jerusalem, and around as far as to Illyricum, I have fully preached the Good News of Christ; ²⁰ yes, making it my aim to preach the Good News, not where Christ was already named, that I might not build on another's foundation. ²¹ But, as it is written,
"They will see, to whom no news of him came.
    They who haven't heard will understand."

²² Therefore also I was hindered these many times from coming to you, ²³ but now, no longer having any place in these regions, and having these many years a longing to come to you, ²⁴ whenever I travel to Spain, I will come to you. For I hope to see you on my journey, and to be helped on my way there by you, if first I may enjoy your company for a while. ²⁵ But now, I say, I am going to Jerusalem, serving the saints. ²⁶ For it has been the good pleasure of Macedonia and Achaia to make a certain contribution for the poor among the saints who are at Jerusalem. ²⁷ Yes, it has been their good pleasure, and they are their debtors. For if the Gentiles have been made partakers of their spiritual things, they owe it to them also to serve them in fleshly things. ²⁸ When therefore I have accomplished this, and have sealed to them this fruit, I will go on by way of you to Spain. ²⁹ I know that when I come to you, I will come in the fullness of the blessing of the Good News of Christ.

³⁰ Now I beg you, brothers, by our Lord Jesus Christ and by the love of the Spirit, that you strive together with me in your prayers to God for me, ³¹ that I may be delivered from those who are disobedient in Judea, and that my service which I have for Jerusalem may be acceptable to the saints, ³² that I may come to you in joy through the will of God, and together with you, find rest. ³³ Now the God of peace be with you all. Amen.

WHY?
What led to the action or dialogue that took place in this passage? Record every question you have about the purpose for what is said or done.

OTHER QUESTIONS & OBSERVATIONS

CONTENT
Record figures of speech, questions and answers, lists, comparisons, etc. What questions do these bring up?

___

CONTEXT
What is the immediate context and the broader context? What happens right before and after this passage?

___

COMPARISON
Track down scripture quotations, compare similar passages, notice other uses in scripture of special terms, names, or ideas.

___

CULTURE
How does the cultural context influence this passage? What questions do you need answered about the culture to understand it better?

CONSULTATION
Explore commentaries and sermons on this passage and record helpful thoughts.

APPLICATION
Keeping in mind the meaning of this passage in its original context, how can you apply this passage to your life?

16 I commend to you Phoebe, our sister, who is a servant of the assembly that is at Cenchreae, ² that you receive her in the Lord, in a way worthy of the saints, and that you assist her in whatever matter she may need from you, for she herself also has been a helper of many, and of my own self. ³ Greet Prisca and Aquila, my fellow workers in Christ Jesus, ⁴ who risked their own necks for my life, to whom not only I give thanks, but also all the assemblies of the Gentiles. ⁵ Greet the assembly that is in their house. Greet Epaenetus, my beloved, who is the first fruits of Achaia to Christ. ⁶ Greet Mary, who labored much for us. ⁷ Greet Andronicus and Junia, my relatives and my fellow prisoners, who are notable among the apostles, who were also in Christ before me. ⁸ Greet Amplias, my beloved in the Lord. ⁹ Greet Urbanus, our fellow worker in Christ, and Stachys, my beloved. ¹⁰ Greet Apelles, the approved in Christ. Greet those who are of the household of Aristobulus. ¹¹ Greet Herodion, my kinsman. Greet them of the household of Narcissus, who are in the Lord. ¹² Greet Tryphaena and Tryphosa, who labor in the Lord. Greet Persis, the beloved, who labored much in the Lord. ¹³ Greet Rufus, the chosen in the Lord, and his mother and mine. ¹⁴ Greet Asyncritus, Phlegon, Hermes, Patrobas, Hermas, and the brothers who are with them. ¹⁵ Greet Philologus and Julia, Nereus and his sister, and Olympas, and all the saints who are with them. ¹⁶ Greet one another with a holy kiss. The assemblies of Christ greet you.

¹⁷ Now I beg you, brothers, look out for those who are causing the divisions and occasions of stumbling, contrary to the doctrine which you learned, and turn away from them. ¹⁸ For those who are such don't serve our Lord, Jesus Christ, but their own belly; and by their smooth and flattering speech, they deceive the hearts of the innocent. ¹⁹ For your obedience has become known to all. I rejoice therefore over you. But I desire to have you wise in that which is good, but innocent in that which is evil. ²⁰ And the God of peace will quickly crush Satan under your feet. The grace of our Lord Jesus Christ be with you.

²¹ Timothy, my fellow worker, greets you, as do Lucius, Jason, and Sosipater, my relatives. ²² I, Tertius, who write the letter, greet you in the Lord. ²³ Gaius, my host and host of the whole assembly, greets you. Erastus, the treasurer of the city, greets you, as does Quartus, the brother. ²⁴ The grace of our Lord Jesus Christ be with you all! Amen. ²⁵

WHY?
What led to the action or dialogue that took place in this passage? Record every question you have about the purpose for what is said or done.

OTHER QUESTIONS & OBSERVATIONS

CONTENT
Record figures of speech, questions and answers, lists, comparisons, etc. What questions do these bring up?

CONTEXT
What is the immediate context and the broader context? What happens right before and after this passage?

COMPARISON
Track down scripture quotations, compare similar passages, notice other uses in scripture of special terms, names, or ideas.

CULTURE
How does the cultural context influence this passage? What questions do you need answered about the culture to understand it better?

_____
_____
_____
_____
_____
_____
_____
_____
_____
_____
_____

CONSULTATION
Explore commentaries and sermons on this passage and record helpful thoughts.

_____
_____
_____
_____
_____
_____
_____
_____
_____
_____
_____
_____
_____
_____

APPLICATION
Keeping in mind the meaning of this passage in its original context, how can you apply this passage to your life?

Made in the USA
Monee, IL
30 August 2023

41852164R00085